KU-299-780

NINE SHARP AND EARLIER

NINE SHARP & EARLIER

Herbert Farjeon

Illustrated by
Anna Zinkeisen

LONDON: J. M. DENT AND SONS LTD

SOME of these verses go better with music, but those who have heard them in *Nine Sharp* and other revues may enjoy the recollection. Acknowledgments are due to my sister Eleanor for her collaboration in the 'Paean to Nature,' and to the proprietors of *Punch*, the *Tatler*, and the *Graphic* (now incorporated with the *Sphere*), for permission to reprint lyrics of which they hold the copyright.

H. F.

CONTENTS

CONTENTS

WHEN BOLONSKY DANCED BELUSHKA

Of ballet fans we are the cream,
  We never miss a night;
The ballet is our only theme,
Our Russian accent is a dream,
We say the name of every *prim-*
  A ballerina right;
The ballet is our meat and drink,
  It is our staff of life,
Our prop, our safety-valve, our link,
Our vice, our passion, foible, kink,
The ballet is, we really think,
  Our mistress and our wife.
        It 's true that many lesser clans
          For ballet also thirst,
        But they are merely *nouveau* fans,
          It 's we who liked it first,
        And we who know it best, becos,
          Ask any *connoisseur*,
        The ballet isn't what it was
          When we were what we were.

          Oh, the urge
          To see Serge!
          What a thrill!
          What a pill!
          I

What a purge!
So adept
When he leapt,
We were dumb,
Overcome,
Overswept!

When Bolonsky danced *Belushka* in September 1910,
  What a wonderful night that was! what a wonderful
    sight that was!
We are positive that nobody has really danced since
    then!
  How pellucid! how light he was! like an angel in
    flight he was!
      He jumped *comme çi*,
      He jumped *comme ça*,
     We can't precisely show you how,
     But when he stamped,
     Ra-ta-ta-ta,
     Well, don't you wish you'd seen him now?
When Bolonsky danced *Belushka* in September 1910,
  How his miming elated us! how his timing pros-
    trated us!
When Bolonsky danced *Belushka*, as we keep on
    saying, when
  He was just at the peak of it! oh, we hardly can
    speak of it!
Something happened then *you'll* never, never, never,
    never see,
So don't talk about these others, but apply your
    mind to me,

And although we 've told you so before, we *must*
  repeat again—
When Bolonsky danced Belushka *in September 1910!*

Though to-day's *Boutique Fantasque* 'll do for Haskell
  and his lot,
  It is not good enough for us! it is rather too
    rough for us!
We miss the old precision, on the beat, and on the dot,
  When Bolonsky attacked a scene in *Giselle* or in
    Lac des Cygnes.
      In *Igor*, too,
      He used to do
    Cataclysmic, cosmic things!
      While in *Sylphides*
      We 're all agreed
    One night *we really saw his wings!*
When Bolonsky danced *Belushka* in September 1910,
  How poetic! how lyrical! what a feat! what a
    miracle!
Oh, the sighing of the women! and the swooning
  of the men!
  When he twiddled and twirled for us, he created
    a world for us!
How we screamed and shrieked and hooted, how we
  whooped and how we howled!
We were ravished and uprooted! we were frankly
  disembowelled!
You will never know the throb, the glow, the bliss
  that we knew then,
When Bolonsky danced *Belushka* in September 1910

HOTEL PIECE

As manageress of the Talbot Arms
    I try to keep the tone up;
I 've a smile that cheers and a voice that charms
    Our visitors when they phone up;
A very good class we cater for
    In tweeds and aquascuta
That don't disgrace our antlers or
    Our sporting prints or pewter.
    My coiffure cannot fail to pass,
        My spray is picturesque,
    My nails are nice, and I keep a glass
        Of stout behind the desk.
It 's true our guests may sometimes fail
    To tip the under-porter,
Our chambermaids could tell a tale
    Or two about hot water,
We sometimes find a lady's comb
    In a bedroom that surprises,
But there! to make a home from home
    It takes all sorts and sizes.

There 's No. 37 who is given to complain,
And No. 5 whose overcoat has lost its collar-chain,
17 is quite a puzzle—I can't think what he 's about—
He keeps on going out and coming in and going out;
No. 12 is so extremely hoity-toity and select

He never says Good Morning, which is *not* what I
  expect,
  And No. 44
  Has forgotten to bring more
Than the top of his pyjamas, which creates a bad effect.
No. 2 is back from Egypt, which is rather more my
  line,
But you can have the lot if you will give me No. 9—
Oh, the leather of his suit-case really gave me such
  a thrill
That every time I see him, I can somehow smell it still;
He's a dozen pair of boots, and he's a dozen pair
  of trees
(You can always tell a gentleman by little things
  like these),
He telephones to Ascot, and he telephones to Cowes—
It's for him I wear these lilies-of-the-valley in my
  blouse.
Oh, No. 9, yes, No. 9 is all the rage with me,
It gives me quite a flutter just to think I have his key,
And his voice! I often mention to him, just to hear
  him speak,
What simply gorgeous weather we experienced last
  week.
He's got a place in Dorking that I gather is divine,
And the extras he has had! the baths! the billiards!
  the wine!
  Oh, I feel that this hotel
  Would do very, very well
If we had a few more clients of the class of No. 9.

B

Our lady guests are apt to be more fussy than the men—
What with draughts and smells and ringing bells, I 'm
sick of No. 10;
That wretched little dog of hers should really be
restrained,
She should keep it in a kennel if she cannot have it
trained.
No. 20 is less bother, but I must confess I hope
Next time she leaves the writing-room, she 'll leave
one envelope—
It 's funny how the *Sphere*
And the *Tatler* disappear!
When she goes away on Friday I quite tremble for
the soap.
But to all these little troubles I most willingly resign,
For after all, there 's always, yes, there 's always No. 9!
I 'll bet he looks a dream when they take in his
morning tea;
He 's A.A. through and through, with not a trace
of C.T.C.;
He is always so agreeable, with a pleasant word to say,
I 'll be quite the Madam Butterfly the day he goes away;
Our little conversations are so chatty and so bright
That I 'm sure he rather likes me—though of course
it 's quite all right.
This morning, when I said the weather really was
a shame,
He said it really was—we somehow always think the
same—
Then he asked me, Was I busy? and I said: 'Just one
long buzz,

But working stops you thinking,' and he answered:
    'Yes, it does!'
And then I looked straight in his eyes, and he looked
    straight in mine,
And I said: 'Well, just for your sake, I do hope it
    comes out fine.'
    Oh, I'm sure that this hotel
    Would do very, very well
If we had a few more clients of the class of No. 9.

PULLING DOWN LONDON

Oh, a fisherman's life is a life that's gay
    As he sails on the open sea,
And a vagabond's life on the great highway
    Is a life that is fine and free,
The steeplejack and the blacksmith black
    Rejoice in their employment,
But a job I've got that tops the lot
    For open-air enjoyment,
            As here
            I stand
    My pick-axe in my hand,
            'Neath God's
            Blue sky
    I make the plaster fly—

Pulling down London, smashing up the town,
    That is the life for me,
A-breaking up of beauty and a-knocking of it down,
    Under the sky so free,
    So whack that roof and bang them walls
    And scatter the old brickbats,
    And down with the Adelphi and the Temple and
        St Paul's,
    And up with the Service Flats,
            By Gee,
    Yes, up with the Service Flats.

10

Sir Christopher Wren was all right then,
  But he ain't no great shakes now,
So drill that drill, my lads, until
  You can't see the dust for row—
The face of the world is changing fast,
But only fossils want things to last,
So shiver the foundations and blast the past
  Pulling down London Town.

If aeroplanes with bombs on high
  Destroyed what I destroy,
Oh, wouldn't there be a great outcry,
  You bet there would, my boy!
If what them Adam Brothers built
  Was bashed by the foe's barrage,
Oh, wouldn't we shout about the guilt
  Of doing it free of charge,
      By Gee,
  Foreign labour free of charge!
But who will grouse if Pembroke House
  Is bust by an Englishman?
Or shake his fist if I assist
  At the death of the best Queen Anne?
There's not much money in the past that's gone,
But there's oodles in a brand-new Odeon,
So civilization marches on
      Pulling down London Town.

SONGS OF THE B.B.C.

THANK GOD FOR THE B.B.C.

THANK God for the B.B.C.,
Thank God for the B.B.C.,
    Through whose kind labours
    We rejoice our neighbours,
Thank God for the B.B.C.

At breakfast, dinner, and tea
We feed with the B.B.C.,
    We munch our pork
    To a King-Hall Talk,
Our sausages to Tchaikovskee.

Wherever we chance to be,
In study or sculleree,
    Our portable set
    Is there, you bet,
Yes, even in the lavatree.

Thank God for the B.B.C.,
Thank God for the B.B.C.,
    So tune in, boys,
    It's an age of noise,
Thank God for the B.B.C.

13

ONLY A CROONER

I 'm only a crooner, dear,
　Who 's crooning to you,
You may prefer a piano-tuner, dear,
　Chacun à son goût——
　　　　　　　　(Goo, goo, goo, goo, goo)
My voice is like honey, dear,
　My lips are like glue—
Don't answer No, think of the money, dear,
　I 've made by crooning to you.

VAUDEVILLE ERIC AND RADIO VAL

BOTH. 　　　Big bugs we
　　　　　　Of the B.B.C.,
　Among the nobs we 're counted,
　　　Higher and higher
　　　In the hierarchee
　Of the B.B.C. we 've mounted,
　Till now in the air we 've got so high
　We feel we are floating through the sky.

ERIC. We 're Vaudeville Eric——
VAL. 　　　　　　　　　and Radio Val——
ERIC. Sing tral-lal-lal-lal——
VAL. 　　　　　　　　tral-lal-lal-lal-lal.
　I have a brother *qui n'est pas très mal*——
ERIC. And I have a wife who 's a dam clever gal.
VAL. My radio plays I can highly commend
　For I listened to one of 'em through to the end.

14

ERIC. A Viennese musical piece with a waltz
Is always O.K., for it never rings false.

VAL. Our names in the papers you 've noticed, no
doubt.

ERIC. We don't know how they get there, we *can't*
keep them out.

BOTH. So sing tral-lal-lal-lal-lal-lal-lal-lal-lal-lal
For Vaudeville Eric and Radio Val.

ERIC. We 're Vaudeville Eric——

VAL. and Radio Val——

ERIC. Sing tral-lal-lal-lal——

VAL. tral-lal-lal-lal-lal.

ERIC. I 'm not in the least little bit Regional.

VAL. Though I haven't played Hamlet, I think that
I shall.

ERIC. I manage to turn out with ardour sublime
The smash hits of Maschwitz all in my spare time.

VAL. Old Shakespeare at last I have put on the map,
Thanks to plenty of trumpets and cutting and snap.

ERIC. Though in some things we differ, in this we 're
alike——

VAL. We make more and more, for we 're both on
the mike——

BOTH. So sing tral-lal-lal-lal-lal-lal-lal-lal-lal-lal,
For Ariel Eric and Prospero Val.

SONGS OF THE B.B.C.

RULER O' THE B.B.C.

When I was a bairn, I dwelt up north
In the Land o' the Leal and the Fairth o' Forth,
And a' through my youth in my ain countree
I polished up my English very carefullee
(*He polished up his English very carefullee*).
I polished up my English sae carefullee
That I became the Ruler o' the B.B.C.
(*He polished up his English sae carefullee
That he became the Ruler o' the B.B.C.*)

I sent for some chaps to gi'e some chats,
And some aunts and uncles tae amuse the brats,
But the best of a' the folk they use
Are the braw bonnie laddies wha' annoonce the news
(*The braw bonnie laddies wha' annoonce the news*).
They say 'Guid nicht' sae beautiflee
A' the lassies are in lo'e wi' the B.B.C.
(*They say 'Guid nicht' sae beautiflee
A' the lassies are in lo'e wi' the B.B.C.*)

That nae man's morals should be lax or loose
I decided when I built Broadcastin' Hoose,
So I summoned up my staff and said: 'Hoot, mon,
    hoot!
If I hear of ye canoodlin', ye gang right oot!'
(*If he hears of us canoodlin', we gang right oot!*)
I sat upon canoodlin' sae successfullee
There's never been a babby in the B.B.C.
(*He sat upon canoodlin' sae successfullee
There's never been a babby in the B.B.C.*)

17

CRUISE, BABY!

CRUISING
On the swell blue ocean,
That's the slap-up notion,
The steamship shout,
Everybody is cruising,
Cruising half-denuded,
Everything included,
First-class throughout.
Tangier, Algiers,
Algier, Tangiers,
And an hour or two in Malta,
Majorc, Minorc,

And a dam quick walk
On the Rock of Gibraltar,
No tips, no fuss,
No snags for us,
No choice, no choosing,
We land as we planned,
Then back we track,
And we go on cruising.

Cruising
With the spinster in the pince-nez
Who isn't really half as fas'cna-
Ting as she thinks—
Isn't Egypt a treat, sweet?

CRUISE, BABY!

If you feel dead beat, sweet,
Come and rest your feet, sweet,
Behind that Sphinx.
What sun-tanned guides!
What well-planned rides
To tombs in hidden places!

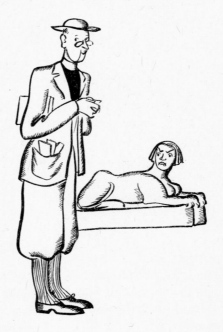

Kismet! what fates!
What figs! what dates!
What camels and oases!
What jars! what pots!
And my! what lots

Of beggars we're refusing!
We land as we planned,
Then back we track,
And we go on cruising!

Cruising
With the spinster in the pince-nez
And the parson in the plus-fours
On the sunshine sea—
Vesuvius is grand, kid,
When I hold you by the hand, kid,
We're in Casanova-land, kid,
And Casanova's me.
What bays! what capes!
What vines! what grapes!

CRUISE, BABY!

What a marvellous Old Master!
What grand remains!
My God! what drains!
Let us walk a little faster!
What fine façades!
What nice post cards!
Look, these are quite amusing!
We land as we planned,
Then back we track,
And we go on cruising.

Cruising
With the spinster in the pince-nez
And the parson in the plus-fours
And the bath-chair case—
Let's go down to the bazaar, babe,
I'll be your passionate pasha, babe,
If you'll just be what you are, babe—
I like this place!
I like that mosque!
That cute kiosk!
That turban and that tunic!
That veiled brunette!
Eyes front, my pet—
You can't get off with a eunuch!
Constantinope
Gives so much scope
It's quite confusing—
We land as we planned,
Then back we track,
And we go on cruising.

Cruising
With the spinster and the parson
And the nurse behind the bath-chair
And the whole dam show—
Greece requires a lot of beating
If you don't mind what you're eating—
How I wish I'd brought some Keating,
They love me so!
What marble gods!
What bronze tripods!
Yes, my soul at last has woken!
What sea! what sand!
What statues! and
What a pity they're all broken!
This Parthenon
Is too far gone—
It's no longer fit for using—
We land as we planned,
Then back we track,
And we go on cruising.

THEME SONGS FOR SHAKESPEARE

I

TITANIA,
You 've made a hit, Titania,
I 've got a mania,
Titania,
For you.
On mossy banks, dear,
Where Mister Puck plays pranks, dear,
I 'll draw no blanks, dear,
Thanks, dear,
To you.
   About your wings
   And other things
     I 'm absolutely loopy,
   So let your elves
   Amuse themselves
     While we make fairy whoopee—
You 've made a hit, Titania,
You 're full of It, Titania,
You can bet your boots,
If you 'll be my toots,
I 'll never quit Titania.

II

Moody Dane,
Moody Dane,
Why are
You moody?
Broody Dane,
Broody Dane,
Don't be
So broody!
Smile a smile, dear,
Dry your eyes,
Try not to
Soliloquize,
Don't keep sayin':
'That's the question,'
It is only
Indigestion—
Moody Dane,
Moody Dane,
Don't be
So naughty!
It is all
Wrong to call
Your Momma
Bawdy—
There's a bend in every lane,
Soon the sun will shine again,
Skies of blue come after rain,
Moody Dane,
Moody Dane.

III

Lordee!
Lordee!
I may be black,
But I 'm feelin' yellow,
All day I cry: 'Alack,
Alack, Othello!'
It 's true my Desdemona 's hide
Is white outside,
But these Venetians
Are chock-full of secretions.

My gal 's leadin' me such a dance,
Farewell to pomp and farewell circumstance!
Farewell, content! I 've got the hump!
Farewell to everything except my trump!

IV

I 'm Rosalind
Of Elstree brand,
They 've got me tinned,
They 've got me canned,
I 'm unsurpassed
In an all-star cast
Of sheep in the Forest of Arden.
Upon the flicks
Mit clowns in smocks
I feed my chicks,
I feed my flocks,

27

Upon the screen
I am the queen
Of the kine in the Forest of Arden.
  The things some people say I 'm like
    Are really rather damping,
  A secondary schoolgirl on the hike,
    Or a little German sausage camping—
When I speak prose,
When I speak verse,
My accent goes
From bad to worse,
But the money I earn
Is *wunderschön*
On the set in the Forest of Arden.

Orlando's ways
Appeal to me,
He carves my praise
On every tree—
What splendid free
Publicitee
For me in the Forest of Arden!
I like to wear
These kind of clothes,
I look so fair
In trunk and hose
I do not care
Not if it snows
All over the Forest of Arden.
  Your English verse, however blank,
    I speak it like a scholiar,

I taught myself, so *Gott sei dank*,
    And nuts to Constance Collier.
Mit legs apart
I speak my bits,
And since my art
Knows no limits,
Ach, *Donner und Blitz*,
I 'll do the splits
In the beautiful Forest of Arden.

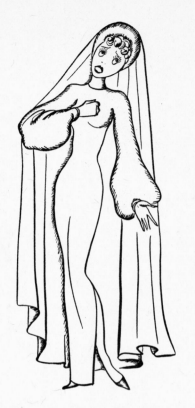

HOLLYWOOD FUNERAL

WEEP!
Weep, all ye film-fans!
Weep, broken-hearted,
For the departed!
Sackcloth and ashes!
Paradise crashes!
Roy Regal is dead!
His spirit has fled!

HOLLYWOOD FUNERAL

Moan!
Virgin and widow!
Typist and heiress!
Midwife and mayoress!
Sour girl and sweet girl!
Good girl and street girl!
Roy Regal's deceased!
His spirit's released!

Never a star
In sky or on earth
Came near to his fame
Since Hollywood's birth!
Never a guy
So desired and adored,
Since Adam was born
Of the breath of the Lord!

Wail!
Wail the world over!
Loud lamentation!
Every nation!
Black, white, and yellow,
Hollow and bellow!
Roy Regal bemoan!
His spirit has flown!

No more his Roman swimming-pool he'll swim in,
　Or steer his Chinese junk 'neath starry skies,
No more on blinding sunbleached women
　His sex-appeal he'll exercise.

No more in his Renaissance villa
  Prime Ministers and poets he 'll entertain,
No more, no more his pet gorilla
  Shall squat beside him in his monoplane.

In pearl and onyx coffin now are laid out
  The lovely limbs the world admired,
Roy Regal 's dead, he 's done his final fade-out,
  His contract on this earth 's expired.

Plunged in despair are his adherents,
  Disconsolate, enwrapped in woe,
He 's gone to make a personal appearance
  In Heaven where all good stars go.

        No one could sing
        A Mother song
        Like Roy could,
        No one could wring
        Your heart like that
        Big boy could,
        When he sang 'Mammy,
        I want my Mammy,
        Darling old Mammy,
        Mammy, I want you
        Bad,
        So bad.'
        No one could make
        Your bosom heave
        Like Roy did,
        No one could break

Your heart like that
Big boy did,
When he sang 'Mammy,
I want my Mammy,
Darling old Mammy,
Mammy, I want you
Bad,
So bad.'

Moan!
Virgin and widow!
Typist and heiress!
Midwife and mayoress!
Sour girl and sweet girl!
Good girl and street girl!
Roy Regal bemoan!
His spirit has flown!

Weep!
Weep, all ye film-fans!
Weep, broken-hearted,
For the departed!
Sackcloth and ashes!
Paradise crashes!
His spirit has fled!
Roy Regal,
Roy Regal is dead!

LOOKING AT THE STARS

LOOKING at the stars
And holding hands
In the cinemas
Or on the sands.
Mickey Mouse or Mars,
It's all the same to us,
What's in a name to us?

34

What Frances Day?
The Milky Way?
King Charles's Wain? or
Janet Gaynor?
Stars upon the screen
Or in the sky
Serve as a conven-
Ient alibi—
Something to have seen
And talk about again
When we 've been out again—
The Great North Light
And Conrad Veidt
Both have their uses
As excuses.

Jessie, do you
Realize
When you use those
Baby eyes,
Smile those smiles, or
Sigh those sighs,
You 're really only playing gooseberry?
Constance, though you
Play with fire
As a daughter
Of desire
All dressed up in
Night attire,
You 're really only playing gooseberry.

35

Robert Taylor, any night
When we 'd be alone,
Comes in handy as a quite
Useful chaperone—
Claudette when she
Flirts with sin,
Gloria on that
Tiger-skin,
Even Venus
Must agree,
Shining down on
You and me,
Queen of Love though
She may be,
She 's really only playing gooseberry.

CARTES POSTALES

AND now, for your content,
We venture to present
Des *tableaux amoureux, et pas si mal,*
Glimpses of tinted art
Appealing to ze heart
Depicted on ze dainty *carte*
Postale.

Before ze stationer's shop
Who is not fain to stop
And gaze when on some Continental tour?
What traveller can feel *triste*
At ze tobacconiste
Before zis cardboard feast
Of gay *amour?*

What rich, what perfumed dreams,
For just a few centimes,
Are ours to set ze senses in a whirl!
Come, zen! and play ze game
Of cards we know by name
As *Jolie Fille, Je t'Aime*
Et Enfin Seuls.

PREMIÈRE CARTE

Je baise, tu baises, nous baisons,
C'est la saison
D'amour, chérie!   (*Ah, Gaston!*)

37

"BONNE ANNÉE"

N'y a personne dans la maison,
Quel délicieux liaison,
Baisons, baisons, baisons,
    Baisons, chérie!   (*Ah, Gaston!*)
Tes oreilles, tes cheveux, tes lèvres,
  Ton épaule, ton nez, ton cou,
Comme porcelaine de Sèvres,
  Oo, oo, chérie! oo, oo!   (*Ah, Gaston!*)
N'y a personne dans la maison,
Quel délicieux liaison,
Baisons, baisons, baisons,
    Baisons, baisons, chérie!   (*Ah, Gaston!*)

We next invite a peep,
Bon marché, very cheap,
At *une espèce de carte postale intime.*
I tell you *vraiment* zat
All hearts go pit-a-pat
Each time zat zey look at
    Zis dainty dream.

DEUXIÈME CARTE

Joli garçon, c'est moi, oui, oui,
Et j'ai beaucoup de jolis amis,
  Jolis amis, jolis amis,
Et j'ai beaucoup de jolis amis.

Regardez bien ces jolies fleurs,
Envoyées par un joli monsieur,
  Joli monsieur, joli monsieur,
Envoyées par un joli monsieur.

Regardez bien ces jolies roses,
Si symbolique de quelque chose,
Quelque chose, quelque chose,
Si symbolique de quelque chose.

Joli garçon, c'est moi, oui, oui,
Et j'ai beaucoup de jolis amis,
Jolis amis, jolis amis,
Et j'ai beaucoup de iolis amis.

To conclude zis display,
Ohé, ohé, ohé,
Attendez donc a song you all have sung
When you were innocent,
Though you, of course, dident
Know what it really meant,
You were so young.

TROISIÈME CARTE

Josephine, Josephine,
Dormez-vous? dormez-vous?—
Non, je peux pas dormir,
Non, je peux pas dormir,
Ding-dong-boo!
Ding-dong-boo!

Josephine, Josephine!—
Entrez-vous! entrez-vous!

Qu'est-ce que vous attendez?
Qu'est-ce que vous attendez?
Ding-dong-boo!
Ding-dong-boo!

Josephine, Josephine,
Voulez-vous? voulez-vous?—
Soufflez la chandelle!
Soufflez la chandelle!
Ding-dong-boo!
Ding-dong-boo!

SWEET NELL,
NEAT NELL

FOR years and years the public
Has hailed with happy hoots
My snappy little jumper
And elastic-sided boots,
For years and years I've been
  a pro,
I've still got all my teeth,
I'm fairly well preserved
  outside
And not bad underneath.

  Sweet Nell! neat Nell! the
    dream-girl of the halls!
  They hear me! they cheer
    me! and oh, the curtain-
    calls!
  What gags! hot gags! all
    the stalls in fits!
  Oh, what a wonderful life
    I've had—hits! hits! hits!

THE LAST OF ENGLAND

For the picture by Ford Madox Brown

MAN.   The day has come at last,
        The day for sailing,
    For cutting adrift from the past
        That was nothing but failing—
    Now it is time to try
        New hope, new endeavour,
    Now it is England good-bye,
        Good-bye for ever.
                (All aboard! all aboard!)
Good-bye to the fields we have loved, good-bye
    to the lanes,
Good-bye to the gates, and the roofs, and the sun
    on the window-panes,
Good-bye to the bricks in the walls, to the smoke
    that ascends
From the chimney-stacks of the homes of our life-
    long friends.
                      (All aboard!)
Good-bye to the earth we have crumbled in our
    hand,
Good-bye to the streets and the cities we know
    and understand,
To the woods we have wandered through in the
    fading light,

To the birds that have sung as we lay in our beds
at night.

WOMAN. The house stands empty now,
      The rooms are bare,
    I can hear the boots of the men
      On the hollow stair,
    And the horse that whinnied high
      In the waiting cart—
    The blanks where the pictures hung
      Are a blank in my heart.

MAN. There is work, they say, beyond, and a world
    that's new
For those who have failed at home in the task that
    they strove to do—
Good-bye to our native land, to our native sky,
To the life that is ended now. England, good-bye.
                (*All aboard! all aboard!*)

L'ABSINTHE

For the picture by Dégas

PARIS in spring,
Spring in the air,
Birds on the wing
Everywhere—
They 'll all find out one day
There 's nothing to find out.
Spring in the sky,
Every one
Goes gladly by
In the sun—
They 'll all find out one day
There 's nothing to find out.
    Nothing to sigh for,
    Nothing to fear,
    Nothing to care for at all,
    Nothing to die for,
    Just to sit here
    Watching the sun on the wall—
Paris in May,
Spring in the sound
Of children playing around—
They 'll all find out one day
There 's nothing to find out.

Garçon! encore!
Did you see Jacques lately?
I never liked him greatly,
He was so overstrung.
Bertrand was more—
Well, in a way, attentive,
But, *mon Dieu!* inventive!
What a clever tongue!
  Just let him once begin,
  You had to listen to him,
  He never took me in
  Or knew I saw through him,
  Still, it was quite all right—
  I somehow knew him
    To be my kind,
    I didn't mind,
    I was resigned!
Mean little eyes,
And when he used to pat me,
He didn't look straight at me
As he did before. . . .
Was I quite wise,
When it was clearly ending,
To let him keep pretending? . . .
Garçon! encore!

Garçon! encore!
What has become of Louis?
I wonder if it's true he
Can be really dead?
Is he still sore

46

L'ABSINTHE

About the way I slipped him
After I had stripped him,
Or so people said?
   I never liked that cough,
   I was apprehensive,
   Nothing could keep it off
   And it came expensive—
   Life was too grim with him,
   Yes, too intensive,
     It was a strain,
     For all that pain
     Drove me insane. . . .
Still, he was nice
I 'd rather like to meet him,
Though I dare say I 'd treat him
As I did before—
   Just once or twice
   I thought he might get better,
   But when I saw that letter. . . .
   Garçon! encore!

Paris in spring—
Green on the trees—
Let lovers sing
As they please,
They 'll all find out one day
There 's nothing to find out.
Spring is a call
That signifies
Nothing at all
To the wise—

47

They 'll all find out one day
There 's nothing to find out.
    Nothing to sigh for,
    Nothing to fear,
    Nothing to care for at all,
    Nothing to die for,
    Just to sit here
    Watching the sun on the wall—
Paris in May,
Spring in the sound
Of children playing around—
They 'll all find out one day
There 's nothing to find out.

CHARGE OF THE LATE BRIGADE

Here we come, here we come,
The Always Late Brigade!
Clash the cymbal! beat the drum!
What a scrimmage! what a scrum!
Though we may be troublesome,
We must be obeyed!
Vainly let the mummer mum
When we're on parade!

Bark the shin and bruise the toe!
Knock the knee as in you go!
Jab the elbow in the eye!
Shout a loud apology!
Seek the sixpence! crush the feet!
Block the view and bang the seat!

None shall stop the nightly raid
Of the Always Late Brigade!

Journalists for ever cry
We should be suppressed!
Managers intend to try
By-and-by-and-by-and-by!
But while punctuality
Is a mere request,
Nothing shall effectively
Speed the coming guest!

Graze the ankle! rip the skirt!
Kick the calf and mind you hurt!
When you've got your victim pinned,
Let him have it in the wind!
Settle loudly in your seats!
Beckon for a box of sweets!
Shout for change to be conveyed!
That's the Always Late Brigade!

So once more we loudly sing,
Fold the coat and twang the spring!
Stand and chatter with your host!
Sit, and then play General Post!
Scan the programme! strain the sight!
Ask your neighbour for a light!
Such the game that's nightly played
By the Always Late Brigade!

BEARDS

WE used to be clean-shaven,
Our chins were once quite bald,
  But in our set
  The men we met
Were somehow not enthralled;
When we expressed opinions
On Art and things like that,
  We found the rest
  Quite unimpressed,
The things we said fell curiously flat—

  And so
We grew our beards,
Impressive beards,
Progressive beards,
  And then
We bought some shirts,
Aesthetic shirts,
Synthetic shirts,
And now our friends defer to everything that we
    assert—
You do not need the Brains if you 've the Beard and
    you 've the Shirt.

  Our judgment on Art is
  Respected at parties—

You can say: 'Good law!
What! Evelyn Waugh!'
If you 've a beard,
A brainy beard.
Your disapprobation
Needs no explanation—
Just drawl out your voice
And say: 'Poor James Joyce!'
If you 've a beard,
A brainy beard.
Black beards, brown beards, long beards, short,
Beards of every shape and sort,
All help to flatter
A young man's grey matter—
You can talk no end of rot,
Say the Sitwells should be shot,
Or that A. P. Herbert 's not
Half as funny as his yacht,
Swear that Gollancz is a Scot,
Rose Macaulay stole her plot
From an old *Forget-Me-Not*—
They 'll believe the blooming lot
If you 've a beard.

Impressions overwhelming
With whiskers we create—
However wee,
A nice goatee
Will often carry weight;
Oh, we are very downy

In more than one respect,
    So burn your boats,
    Old nanny-goats,
And come and join the ranks of the elect—

    For you
Will be revered
Once you have reared
A brainy beard,
    And don't
Forget the shirt,
Magnetic shirt,

Prophetic shirt,
And girls with aspirations will be flattered while they
flirt—
You do not need the Sex if you 've the Beard and
you 've the Shirt.

Our burgeoning fringes
Are worshipped at binges—
You can say: 'What! Wells?
Is it true he sells?'
If you 've a beard,
A brainy beard.
Your disapprobation
Needs no explanation—
Just make a little *moue*
And say: 'Bernard Who?'
If you 've a beard,
A brainy beard.
Small beards, big beards, coarse, refined,
Beards of every sort and kind,
All help to flatter
A young man's grey matter.
You can murmur Conrad Veidt
Is a curious kind of blight,
T. S. Eliot cannot write,
Wyndham Lewis isn't quite,
Einstein—well, he 's rather slight,
Glyndebourne's getting rather trite,
White is black and black is white—
And they 're bound to think you right
If you 've a beard.

LIBERTY HALL

I've started a school called Liberty Hall
    Upon the latest system;
We take them big, we take them small,
    And we try not to mould or twist 'em;
Repression is the great pitfall,
    Of this we live in terror,
So we do our best to do nothing at all,
    Lest we should commit some error.

We don't have lessons, we don't have sports,
We don't have rules of any sorts,
And the boys and the girls write their own reports
    In Liberty Hall, the free school;
We don't encourage, we don't suppress,
We don't say No, we don't say Yes,
And when we want, we just undress
    In Liberty Hall, the free school.
        We all abhor
        A dictator,
And sex is quite unshrouded,
        We never, never lock
        The bathroom door—
Last night it was simply crowded—
We do just what we think is nice,
The girls play poker, the boys play dice,
Last week I let them cane me twice
    In Liberty Hall, the free school.

By educating in a modern way
  My reputation made is
Among the intelligentsia,
  The intelligents and ladies;
So send your boy to do my stuff,
  My method can't be beaten,
And then, when I 've saved up enough,
  I 'll send my boy to Eton.

We let them do just what they feel,
We let them swear, we let them steal,
And we don't cut the cards before we deal
        In Liberty Hall, the free school;
We let things slide, we let things rip,
We all gather round to see the matron strip,
We wouldn't spoil the tar for a ha'porth of ship
        In Liberty Hall, the free school.
            It 's true at first
            We feared the worst,
      Our pupils were so frisky,
            But now, when a child
            Displays a thirst,
      We write in the Extras: 'Whisky'—
We let them bill, we let them coo,
But we do just teach them, I fear, it 's true,
What the Woman who Lived in a Shoe never knew
        At Liberty Hall, the free school.

DIRTY SONGS

EVERY night in
Cabaret
On my stool I
Sit and play,
Entertaining
Slap-up throngs
With dirty, dirty,
Dirty songs.
Dirty songs in
Clean hotels,
That 's the way to
Milk the swells,
All the smart folk
Simply long
For a dirty, dirty,
Dirty song.

The bees and the breeze and the trees, no doubt,
  Are well enough now and then,
But when girls who are really girls go out
  With men who are really men,
         What they want
         Is a posh hotel
         Where the food is fresh
         And the songs all smell—
         They feel there must be
         Something wrong

If they don't get a dirty,
Dirty song.

Adam and Eve they
Had no cake
Till Eve she met a
Dirty snake,
They didn't know what was
Right or wrong
Till the snake he sang her a
Dirty song.
Dirty songs with a
Sexy trend
Make folk feel they are
Real West End,
There isn't a thing goes
Down so strong
As a really dirty,
Dirty song.
To the bees and the breeze and the trees, no doubt,
A kitchenmaid heart responds,
But when men who are really men go out
With blondes who are really blondes,
You give 'em smut,
You give 'em dirt,
In a nice white tie
And a nice white shirt,
And they 'll clap you loud,
They 'll clap you long,
Till you give 'em a dirtier
Dirty song.

THANK GOD THAT I'M AN ENGLISHMAN

THANK God, thank God for the Englishman!
Thank God for the pluck and grit he's got!
You always can rely upon the Englishman,
For the Englishman is always on the spot!
Thank God the air I breathe is English air!
Thank God the sod I tread is English sod!
Thank God, thank God that I'm an Englishman!
Thank God, thank God, thank God!

Thank God, thank God for Bulldog Beresford!
For the boys who march in red and those in blue!
For our little English home on its patch of English
    loam!
And thank God for all English mothers too!
Thank God the air I breathe is English air!
Thank God the sod I tread is English sod!
Thank God, thank God that I'm an Englishman!
Thank God, thank God, thank God!

LONG-ON BLUES

FEELING sort of lonesome,
Feeling sort of blue,
Loafing in the long-field
All day through,
Stranded on the boundary,
Waiting for a whack,
Two steps this way,
Two steps back.
What a recreation!
What a game to play!
Maiden after maiden
Never comes my way!
Still I mustn't grumble,
Nobody's to blame,
So here's three cheers
For our National Game!

I've got those Long-On Blues,
    Yes, umpire,
I've got those Long-On Blues.
The batsman's dozing inside his crease,
The bowler's posing in perfect peace—
    It's just an awful bore,
        This team-work—
    It seems to me much more
        Like dream-work—

LONG-ON BLUES

The crowd 's dejected, the scorer snores,
And I 'm expected to save the fours!
Oh, for a pillow to go to sleep!
No wonder, willow, they say you weep!
   Don't care if we win,
   Don't mind if we lose,
   For oh—dear—
I 've got those Long-On Blues.

Fielding in the long-field,
Might be in my grave,
Not a catch to run for,
Not a four to save,
Watching how the daisies
Toil not but are slack—
Two steps this way,
Two steps back.
What a recreation!
Isn't it sublime!
Hitching up your trousers
Just to pass the time!
Still I mustn't grumble,
Nobody 's to blame,
So here 's three cheers
For our National Game!

I 've got those Long-On Blues,
   Yes, umpire,
I 've got those Long-On Blues.
If they keep sitting upon the splice,
I 'll take to knitting, or breeding mice.

I wish the bell for tea
  Would tinkle—
I feel like R.I.P.
  Van Winkle—
If they keep blocking, I'll feed the birds,
Or darn a stocking, or do cross-words!
Oh, for a pillow to go to sleep!
No wonder, willow, they say you weep!
  Don't care if we win,
  Don't mind if we lose,
  For oh—dear—
I've got those Long-On Blues.

TESSA, VANESSA, AND EGBERT

ONE, two, three
Highbrows we,
    Tessa,
    Vanessa,
    And Egbert;
Choice and chaste
In our taste,
    Tessa,
    Vanessa,
    And Egbert;
We can only bear the best,
Bach and Wagner we detest,
Masefield has no true technique,
Gilbert Murray should learn Greek;
    Bernard Shaw
    We abhor,
    Tessa,
    Vanessa,
    And Egbert;
    H. G. Wells
    Somehow smells
    To Tessa,
    Vanessa,
    And Egbert;
Aldous Huxley we 've dismissed
As a sentimentalist,
Poor old Epstein's in a rut,
John is worse than Sickert, BUT

We *do* like Mickey,
Oh, we *do* like Mickey,
Yes, we *do* like Mickey-Mickey Mouse!
He's so fundamental!
And so transcendental!
So intensive!
Comprehensive!
And so *very* inexpensive!
We've exploded D. H. Lawrence,
We are through with Rome and Florence,
And Stravinsky—well, you might as well say Strauss!
And the classic composition
Philistines applaud in Titian
Is not a patch on Mickey-Mickey Mouse!

As a clique
We're unique,
Tessa,
Vanessa,
And Egbert;
We arrange
To be strange,
Tessa,
Vanessa,
And Egbert;
Our relationships appear
To outsiders rather queer,
Still, although we live *à trois*,
Mal y pense qui hon y soit!
What we do
Must be new

To Tessa,
Vanessa,
And Egbert;
We 're above
Common love,
Tessa,
Vanessa,
And Egbert;
Sitting on each other's knee,
We discuss psychology,
We talk Freud instead of smut,
Even that is boring, BUT

We *do* like Mickey,
Oh, we *do* like Mickey,
Yes, we *do* like Mickey-Mickey Mouse!
He 's so exoteric!
And he 's *so* generic!
And so dext'rous—
Deeply dext'rous—
And we 're *sure* he 's ambisextrous!
We have done with Keats and Shelley,
We have seen through Botticelli,
And we wouldn't have a Goya in the house!
While Whistler, Watts, and Watteau,
Giorgione and Giotto
Were not a patch on Mickey-Mickey Mouse!

ROCK-BOTTOM BLONDES

WE may not be vivacious,
Or surprisingly sagacious,
But we 're strictly orchidaceous,
    And we 're blondes,
    Blinding blondes.
We may be over-rated,
And not very animated,
But we 're highly chromium-plated,
    And we 're blondes,
    Bedrock blondes.
  Our minds are null and void,
  But though we 're empty in the head,
  We smile when we suspect

That something witty has been said;
It 's not for conversation
We are taken here and there,
What fascinates the men
And makes them lavish, is our hair.
When supping at the Dorchester,
    A handy place to meet,
We 've nothing much to say,
    But we have lots and lots to eat!
We can choose just what we please on
The menu, so we freeze on
To whatever 's out of season,
    For we 're blondes,
    Blinding blondes.

We work to keep our station
With unflagging application,
It 's a whole-time occupation
    Being blondes,
    Blinding blondes.
Our knowledge is extensive
Of whatever is expensive,
And our claims are comprehensive,
    For we 're blondes,
    Bedrock blondes.
    With city men in lounges,
    With college boys in cars,
    We sit as cold as marble,
    And as silent as cigars,
    And though they sometimes clasp us
    In a passionate embrace,

We assure you, when they 've finished,
Not a hair is out of place.
We like the cheques they give us,
But we notice all the same
That somehow on the counterfoil
They don't fill in our name—
Still, we do not stop to ponder,
We just cash the cheque, and wander
To our coiffeur, to get blonder,
For we 're blondes,
Basic blondes,
Bedrock, rock-bottom blondes.

WIRELESS ANNOUNCER

Used to worship actors,
Used to worship stars,
Used to wait at stage-doors
By their motor-cars,
Then I fell a victim
To a movie-man,
I became a raving, craving
Valentino fan,
Till I changed and made another choice—
Now it's not a Man, it's just a Voice.

Wireless Announcer!
Perfect pronouncer!
I worship you!
(*Voce, not out,* 2)

72

When you begin it,
Your Bulletin it
    Thrills me all through!
    (*Arsenal drew*)
That oh-so-civilized inflexion
Sets me a-quiver with affection
As you predict with circumspection
(*An anti-cyclone moving in a westerly direction*).
    It is no fiction
    Your Oxford diction
        Goes to my head!
        (*Depression will spread*)
    You are so kind and
    Nice and refined and
        Beautifully bred!
        (*Archbishop said*)
I dream when I am alone, dear,
One sweet night you will intone, dear,
In the voice that's all your own, dear,
(*Good night everybody, but particularly Joan, dear!*).

When Sir Walford Davies
Talks it is a joy,
But I wouldn't really
Want him for my boy;
Stephen King-Hall's lectures
Leave me edified,
Yet I've truly no unruly
Wish to be his bride,
Since the sound in which I most rejoice
Is your well-creased super-vellum voice.

Wireless Announcer!
Perfect pronouncer!
  Hark to my pulse!
  (*Racing Results*)
If you but knew, dear,
When I hear you, dear,
  Just how I feel!
  (*This Week's Appeal*)
Oh, how I tremble with elation,
Stirred by your smooth articulation,
As you impart the information
(*The Premier made a statement on the present situation*).
  This oscillating
  Keeps on creating
    Shrieks of distress.
    (*One S.O.S.*)
  What heart could harden
  When you beg pardon,
    Murmuring soft
    (*Sorry I coughed*).
Still, I dream when I 'm alone, dear,
One sweet night you will intone, dear,
In the voice that 's all your own, dear,
(*Good night everybody, but particularly Joan, dear!*).

74

BRONTË SISTER BLUES

THREE little Brontë
    Sisters we,
Strumming as glum
    As glum can be
The Brontë Blues
    In a minor key,
Emily, Charlotte, Anne,
    Sing, sisters!
Emily, Charlotte, Anne.

75

We used to dwell
  In a parsonage,
But now we 've gone
  Upon the stage
Our Sister Act
  Is all the rage,
Emily, Charlotte, Anne,
  Sing, sisters!
Emily, Charlotte, Anne.

    When we sing our blues,
      The Brontë Blues,
    The Brontë fans
      Line up in queues,
    If you 're feeling gay
      Or feeling glad,
    Just count on us
      To make you sad,
      Sing, sisters!

In dismal dumps
  And dolesome gloom
We drag through life
  Till we meet our doom,
So here 's hydy-ho
  For the Brontë boom
In Emily, Charlotte, Anne,
  Sing, sisters!
  Sing, sisters!
Emily, Charlotte, Anne.

Anne cantat.

The more the merrier,
    That 's what the folk all say,
The more the merrier,
    Sentiment sounds O.K.,
But I 've got a sort of a
    Hunch we should change it for
The moor the gloomier
    When it 's a Yorkshire moor.

Charlotte cantat.

I told the world what Jane Eyre did
  (*What Jane Eyre did, what Jane Eyre did!*).
Oh, boy, that jane was sure some kid
  (*Though she called herself a governess!*).
She seemed as chaste as any nun,
But she was bought by every one,
She looked stone cold as a governess should,
But her circulation it was mighty good
  (*And she called herself a governess!*).
'One and one make two,' said Governess Eyre,
'But they may make three if you don't take care,'
And all the boys in town, I guess,
Asked her to be their governess
  (*So she called herself their governess!*).

Emily cantat.

Couldn't say
Why they chose to call the play
Wild Decembers—

77

Why not April, May,
Or Septembers?
Wild weather all year through,
Month after month we 're blue.
Life is hell
Up in Yorkshire where we dwell,
Hellish weather,
While we write our books
All together,
Wind whistling in the flue,
Walls that the damp comes through.
When the world is grey and when the skies are
    frowning,
Out across the moor we run and risk a drowning,
Wish that we could run as long as Mrs Browning,
But, since that 's hard to do,
        For a scoop
        We 've become the Brontë Troupe,
        Brontë Cuties,
        Singing poop-a-doop
        Our long suit is,
        Poop-a-doop in revue,
        Poop-a-doop in revue.

KING'S PROCTOR BLUES

NIGHT after night
I wait and wait,
Lonely and quite
Disconsolate,
All the night through
Resolute to
Preserve my good repute,
Waiting for my
Decree nisi
To be made absolute—

79

I 've got those King's Proctor Blues,
   O Proctor!
Those durn King's Proctor Blues!
You never know where he is for certain,
Under the bed or behind the curtain,
Waitin' to spring if he finds you flirtin',
   O Proctor!
I 've got those King's Proctor Blues!
   O Proctor!
Say, have you heard the news?
Pamela's hopes have all gone spinning,
She 's got to start from the very beginning,
She 's more rescinded against than sinning,
   O Proctor!
   King's Proctor Blues!

I 've got those King's Proctor Blues,
   O Proctor!
Those durn King's Proctor Blues!
Six weary months and nothin' doin'
Makes a girl dream day and night of ruin,
Next time I 'm damned if I 'll do the suein',
   O Proctor!
I 've got those King's Proctor Blues!
   O Proctor!
Mindin' my P's and Q's!
I get so lonesome, sitting, sighing,
If the King's Proctor comes around spying,
Well, he 's a man, and there 's no harm trying—
   O Proctor!
   King's Proctor Blues!

LITERARY WIDOWS

Literary widow,
Mourning in black and white,
Shovel the dust on your old man's coffin
An' sit right down an' write.
Literary widow,
Now no more a wife,
Sit right down in the burial-groun'
An' start your old man's life.

1ST WIDOW. My man was a poet of note.
2ND WIDOW. Mine was a novelist, novels he wrote.
3RD WIDOW. Mine was a dancer, none could float
Through the air like my man.
1ST WIDOW. Mine was shy as a shy gazelle.
2ND WIDOW. Mine had secrets he shrank to tell.
3RD WIDOW. Mine couldn't bear to come out of his
shell,
Couldn't bear, not my man.
1ST WIDOW. We were happy when we were wed.
2ND WIDOW. Going was good till they were dead.
3RD WIDOW. On our lives their lustre shed
A sort of reflected glory.
1ST WIDOW. Loud bewailing bygone years,
2ND WIDOW. We beat our breasts beside their biers,
3RD WIDOW. Till a publisher came and dried our tears,
And got us to write their story.

81

Literary widow,
Mourning in black and white,
Shovel the dust on your old man's coffin
An' sit right down an' write.
Literary widow,
Now no more a wife,
Sit right down in the burial-groun'
An' start your old man's life.

1ST WIDOW. My book is direct and daring.
2ND WIDOW. Mine is searching, mine's unsparing.

3RD WIDOW. Mine is full of love and swearing,
   Absolutely true.
1ST WIDOW. I 've got lots of recognition.
2ND WIDOW. I 've established my position.
3RD WIDOW. I 've gone into a fourth edition
   In a month or two.
1ST WIDOW. Never knew that I could write,
   Still, I somehow thought I might
   Sell if I could keep it bright,
      And how they sold it!
2ND WIDOW. Not quite sure if I can spell,
   All the same, I seem to sell,
   For I had a tale to tell,
      And how I told it!
3RD WIDOW. People say that my memoir
   May have gone a bit too far,
   Still, my revelations are
      Quite without equal.
ALL. If good fortune favours me,
   I know what my luck will be,
   I 'll marry another celebritee
      And write a sequel.

   Literary widow,
   Mourning in black and white,
   Shovel the dust on your old man's coffin
   An' sit right down an' write.
   Literary widow,
   Now no more a wife,
   Sit right down in the burial-groun'
   An' start your old man's life.

83

EVEN HITLER HAD A MOTHER

EVERY nation has a patriotic
  Ballad that it loves to sing,
But the consequence is so chaotic,
  Why not try the other thing?
Kindness and consideration 's
  What old Europe seems to miss,
Therefore let the democratic nations
  All join hands and then sing this:

> *Even Hitler had a mother,*
> *Even Mussolini had a ma,*
> *When they were babies they said Goo, goo, goo,*
> *And sucked their thumbs, and got wet through.*
> *Don't be hard upon the Blackshirts,*

They may be rather Swastika,
        But
Even Hitler had a mother
        And
Even Mussolini had a ma.

Though we may get furious with Hitler
   If we 're not of Aryan race,
Let 's remember that when he was littler
   Someone called him Angel-face.
Though we may not idolize the Duce
   When the news gets rather grim,
Someone called him Hoochy-koochy-koochay,
   That was how she humoured him—

   Even Hitler had a mother,
   Even Mussolini had a ma,
   When they were babies they were cross perhaps,
   But all they needed was a change of naps—maps—
   Don't be hard upon the Blackshirts,
   They may be rather Swastika,
           But
   Even Hitler had a mother
           And
   Even Mussolini had a ma.

BEACH PYJAMAS

Like Mexican sailors
Or tropical plants,
In hats that are floppy
And floppier pants
Secured in their places
By belts or by braces,
We go through the paces
Of modern romance.

Beach pyjamas! beach pyjamas!
Once the most exclusive joy!
Beach pyjamas! beach pyjamas!
Now the pride of *hoi polloi*!
Hats as broad as panamamas
Should be worn with beach pyjamas;
Trousers should be worn with fringes
Dyed in tinges fit for binges;
Orange squares and blue triangles
Look extremely nice with bangles,
Young men oscillate with passion
When they see this latest fashion,
And we're happy when they tremble,
Feeling we at last resemble
Heroines of talky dramas
In our bargain beach pyjamas.

G

With an Argentine fervour
No hurricane blights
We bravely exhibit
Our Chili delights,
Like very brown fairies
From far Buenos Aires
Where life never varies
But always excites.

Beach pyjamas! beach pyjamas!
Buzz in every maiden's head!
Beach pyjamas! beach pyjamas!
Make the beach a sort of bed!
Grandpapas and grandmamamas
May condemn our beach pyjamas,
But the blue serge of the eighties
Nowadays quite out of date is—
Sailor collars and white anchors
Aren't the thing for which one hankers
In this age of Rio Ritas,
Corner-houses and two-seaters—
Therefore we bespread the beaches,
Proud to think we look like peaches
Washed up from the far Bahamas
In our bargain beach pyjamas!

MISS SIBERIA

MID the peerless
Chill and cheerless
Peaks that pierce the steely sky,
Mid the glitter
Of the bitter
Steppes that ever seem to sigh,
Premier chosen
From the frozen
Beauties dwelling in this place,
Sleek and slender,
I, in splendour,
Represent my native race.

Miss Siberia!
Miss Siberia!
This weary waste,
These icy spheres,
I long have graced,
Where nothing cheers,
But now I'm placed
Above my peers,
I'm going on a Grand World Tour!
Miss Siberia!
Miss Siberia!
To win the vote
I could not fail,

I struck the note,
I hit the nail,
And now the boat
Is due to sail,
I'm going on a Grand World Tour!
Miss Montenegro must look to her laurels,
Miss Uruguay won't make any stir,
Miss Coral Island will need all her corals
When Miss Siberia spreads her fur.
Miss Siberia!
Miss Siberia!
Though I'm of low
And humble birth,
And half a ko-
Pec's what I'm worth,
I look as though
I own the earth,
I'm going on a Grand World Tour!

Miss Siberia!
Miss Siberia!
I may not read,
I may not write,
I may not feed
My face polite,
But I'll succeed
In shining bright,
I'm going on a Grand World Tour!
Miss Siberia!
Miss Siberia!
I may be pro-

Letarian,
I may be no
Grammarian,
But even so,
Ça fairy ann,
I'm going on a Grand World Tour!
Miss Guatemala will find the world heartless,
Miss Panama will fairly be capsized,
Miss U.S.A. will seem simple and artless
Once Miss Siberia's civilized.
Miss Siberia!
Miss Siberia!
On foreign ground
I'm gonna curse,
And go around
From bad to worse,
Till I am crowned
Miss Universe!
I'm going on a Grand World Tour!

PAEAN TO NATURE

*With apologies to the Nature Poets
of the Eighteenth Century*

I WALKED upon the pleasing hills
    And gazed at the agreeable view;
My bosom with engaging thrills
    Was fluttered through and through;

And as I eyed, with feelings nice,
    The prospect's meritorious face,
Fain had I found some apt device
    To aid the human race.

The grateful fields, the welcome woods,
    The valleys so acceptable,
Chimed in with my propitious moods
    And graced them very well.

The brook, replete with decent glee,
    The placid fountain, trim and tall,
The well-arranged and steady sea,
    The busy waterfall;

The timely hen, the agile dog,
    The lowly yet the cheerful sow,
Her kind, if common, mate, the hog,
    The meditative cow;

PAEAN TO NATURE

The handsome beet, the pretty pea
That nestles coyly in the pod,
The graceful bean—in all we see
The able Hand of God.

What lessons of the punctual sun
Might pensive mortals daily learn!
When life's inviting task is done,
To twilight we return.

Observe the chaste and modest clouds,
How amiably they meet and greet,
Embellishing in tasteful crowds
The sky so blue and neat.

Then note how the persuasive trees
In interesting buds abound,
And scatter them with genteel ease
On the delightful ground.

'Tis Nature's satisfactory art
Attractive morals to instil,
And make the well-contented heart
Lord of the pliant will.

In calm enjoyment of the charms
With which her temperate paths are rife,
Let us still lead, in Nature's arms,
A civil, sober life.

94

TO G. B. S.

Hail to thee, sprightly sage! hail, attic wit,
    Athletically fit,
Who, when a babe, with cry rhetorical,
In the green land of Liffeys and of Boynes,
    Sprang from Hibernian loins
To be the world's Adelphic Oracle!

Prince of Bravado! Potentate of Vaunts!
    Not without taunts,
Not without scorn and scoff and incivility,
When first thou didst embark upon the fight
    To prove black white
Did man condemn thy *vice-versa*tility!

Stern was the conflict, obdurate the foe,
    But those who, long ago,
Called thee an Imp, admit thee now an Emperor!
No more art thou the bear that is a bug,
    For now, without a shrug,
Te salutamus! Sic mutantur tempora!

Mighty Methuselah! many a day has flown
    Since thou upon the throne
Did set the whiskered Scandinavian,
But now those whiskers wither in the bier,
    And we, instead, revere
Thy beard, unshorn but not unshavian!

95

TO G. B. S.

Long may it grow! long on the Picture Page
    Our eyes engage,
Floating like foam upon the ocean,
Where thou, amphibian Fabian, lean and damp,
    Uncowed by crabs or cramp,
Swimmest upon thy back, to keep the world's devotion!

W. G. *LOQUITUR*

GOOD sirs, who sit at home to-night,
And listen in the fading light
To voices floating on the air
From here, from there, from everywhere:
Imagine now that out of space
Comes the deep spirit voice of Grace—
Old W. G.—whose mighty frame
No more shall lumber through the game—
Old W. G.—whose burly beard
No more is seen, no more is feared:
Yet, from my corner in the sky,
When, not unenvious, I descry
Flannels in fashion down below—
When old familiar sounds I know
Float up—the heavy roller's sound
Clanking across the county ground—
The busy whirr no spring forgets
Of cricket balls in cricket nets—
The insect hum of shillings spun,
Silver and black, against the sun—
The call of the pavilion bell,
Tolling its matin summons—well,
Even an angel or two is stirred,
And when the umpire speaks the word,
The first word of the season—'Play!'—
It has my blessing every May.

Sweet May! ah, month beyond compare!
For now you taste the firstlings rare:
The first square cut, the first clean drive,
The first sharp-shooter you survive,
The first fine glance, the first fair guide,
The first good victory for your side:
Sweet May! once more I smell your oil
Smoothing my bat; and press your soil
Under my thumb; once more I feel
The good soft give of pine or deal
Beneath the nails that pierce the boards
In dressing-rooms from Leeds to Lord's:
Sweet May! you hold a thrill apart,
For now the batsman strains his art
To make the loveliest score of all—
A century to a cuckoo's call.
How many, many Mays have burst
Their buds, and spread their boughs, since first
I learned to watch the ball, to wait,
And always hold my bat up straight!
How many Mays, alas! since last
I let the ball at point go past!
No more! no more! above the crowds,
Like a Jehovah in the clouds
I sit, *sans* bat or ball, and dream,
A captain now without a team:
Yet, though I miss, I miss my May,
Happy that other men still play
The game all England flocked to see
When W. G. was W. G.
So then! to business! Now, my lads,

Up with the stumps! on with the pads!
Out with the cap! whose gaudy rings
Will mellow in a few more springs,
And, as the colours fade, proclaim
A real old master of the game.
Come! to the pitch! The field is set.
Caution, remember, till you get
Your eye in. 'Two leg, umpire, please.'
The wicket-keeper bends his knees;
The slips, with swinging arms, lean low,
Hawks for a swoop, three in a row;
Long-off, beside the boundary-track,
Stands with his hands behind his back,
Lolling; the bowler now has spaced
His run; he turns; his fingers taste
The seam, caress the stitch; he comes;
Through the bright air the new ball hums
A delicate, cleaving note; you sight
Against the screen its clear, red flight,
Tense in the sun; and as it spins,
The prologue ends, and play begins.

APOLOGIA

I MAY be faſt, I may be loose,
I may be easy to seduce,
I may not be particular
To keep the perpendicular,
But all my horizontal friends
Are princes, peers, and reverends,
When Tom or Dick or Bertie call
They leave me ſtriċtly vertical.

ON ACTORS

THEY cry, when critics cook their goose:
'That isn't criticism—it's just abuse!'
But where's the actor who, belauded, says:
'That isn't criticism—it's merely praise!'?

ON A SCOFFER AT THE R.A.

'JUST *look* at that daub! what a perfect disgrace!
  The Royal Academy gets worse each visit!
Oh, I 'm *so* sorry—it 's *not* so bad—I 'd lost the place—
  Well, well, well, so that 's a John, is it?'

THE OLD MUSHROOM

THE mushroom-pluckers through the meadow pass
With steps that quicken, eyes that kindle bright
As they espy upon the smooth-cropt grass
Quarry fresh-sprung: here button mushrooms white,
Sweet, short-stalk'd, buxom, hugging tight the ground;
Here soberer circles, with flat satin sheen,
Up-curling at the rim; some faintly brown'd;
Some bold and fleshy; others shy and lean;
Some spindle-shank'd; and some in social clumps
At rakish angles with inviting rumps.

Yet one the mushroom-pluckers overlook:
An old, old mushroom, broken in the back,
Raddled with rain and tatter'd as a book,
Slug-bitten, insect-ridden, blowzy, black.
Despis'd, deserted in his grassy cave,
Him soon the frost shall nip, the storm shall chill;
Around him shall the winds of winter rave,
Whistling in vain their threnody; until
Snow falls; and then no mushroom more serene,
More white, more perfect, shall the year have seen.

IN PRAISE OF THE NINETIES

Ah, was it forty years ago
A small boy in a sailor-suit
Stole down the path to pick the fruit,
While, in the silent afternoon,
A barrel-organ ground a tune—
The very tune this organ in the Square
Rattles to-day with such a melancholy air?

I never thought, when I was young,
The Man who Broke the Bank would play
Such havoc in my heart one day—
I never thought that round the head
Of *Daisy, Daisy* there would spread
A golden nimbus—or that in the street
Ta-ra-ra-boom-de-ay would sound so strangely sweet.

I never thought, when I was young,
The man who turned the handle round
Would draw me, with his clattering sound,
Back to my single-wicket days,
When Buffalo Bill was all the craze,
And Briggs bowled slows, and Patti sang to
swells,
And Henry Irving sawed the limelight in *The
Bells*.

Jog on, jog on, old Atlas bus!
I think I see thy horses twain
Lumbering townward once again—
Again the driver whoas his nags
For City men with Gladstone bags—

Again they climb the steps to hear his views
On cabs and Kruger and the shocking price of booze.

Jog on, jog on, dear chariot,
Behind whose glass the eye perceives
Twelve ladies with tremendous sleeves—

Some groping for the pocket where
They hide the purse that holds the fare—
Some half-asleep—and one upon whose knee
There jolts, ashamed of youth, the child I used to be.

Or, in a shiny hansom cab,
Hailed by my father from the rank,
We'd helter-skelter to the Bank,
Cutting the corners like a knife,
With bells that clinked a careless life,
And wheels rotating at a rate so brisk
I sometimes wondered was it really worth the risk?

Barmaids, they say, were barmaids then—
But I was young and knew them not.
The decadent poet with his pot
Would loll and contemplate their hips,
But while he looked them in the lips,
Blind to his love, I'd clamour for my swag—
'A sponge-cake and a bath bun in a paper bag.'

Gone are the thighs of yesteryear,
The barmaid's bust, the spacious poise
And convex charms of Panto Boys
Who won male hearts because o' nights
They'd plenty to put in their tights.
Victorian bosoms now are food for jest,
We choose Aladdin for her billiard-table chest.

Gone are the days when tales rang true,
And knickerbocker boys would feed
On Henty and on T. B. Reed—

When pictures, too, provoked a thrill
Unconscious of the painter's skill,
And hearts would leap and pupils would enlarge
As they beheld dear Lady Butler's latest Charge.

Who heeded then the world's mishaps?
Lightly we heard of out-of-works,
And Greeks at bloody war with Turks,

Lightly we viewed the Dreyfus case,
Or Oscar's unexplained disgrace—
And yet it stunned the sight and shocked the brain
To hear the Great Wheel at Earl's Court had stopped
     again!

For tragedy begins at home—
And tragedy would fill my head
When I was early sent to bed,
Where, lying tearless in the light,
With bitter heart and uncontrite,
I'd listen to the garden, till I could
Hear the clear ringing calls of children who were good.

'I'm "he."' . . . 'Look out!' . . .'Yes, honour
     bright!' . . .
'I can't quite reach it!' . . . 'Try the rake!' . . .
'Here's father!' . . . 'What did Stoddart
     make?' . . .
Till, in the artificial day,
An organ would begin to play
The *Intermezzo*, languorously slowed,
Followed by *Knocked 'em in the Old Kent Road*.

But now the charm will work no more . . .
A harsh loud-speaker in the square
Intrudes a less remembered air,
And not for me, ah! not for me
This heartless *Island of Capri*
That puts an end to memory's hide-and-seek
And steals the rose from lovely Lily Langtry's cheek.

IN PRAISE OF THE NINETIES

Yet sweet one day for other men,
Now little boys who watch the skies
With wondering and wakeful eyes,
Sweet, though they hardly know they hear
This tune that steals into the ear,
This *Island of Capri*, that will at last
Echo the ever-young unconquerable past.